Science Technology Engineering Math
STEM STARTERS FOR KIDS

ARTIFICIAL INTELLIGENCE

ACTIVITY Book

Written by Sam Hutchinson

Illustrated by Ste Johnson

FOR YOUNG READERS

Racehorse for Young Readers books may be purchased in bulk at special discounts for sales promotions, corporate gifts, fund-raising or education purposes. Special editions can also be created to specifications. For details, contact the Special Sales Department at Skyhorse Publishing, 307 West 36th Street, 11th Floor, New York, NY 10018 or info@skyhorsepublishing.com.

Racehorse for Young Readers™ is a pending trademark of Skyhorse Publishing, Inc.®, a Delaware corporation.

Visit our website at www.skyhorsepublishing.com.
Please follow our publisher Tony Lyons on Instagram @tonylyonsisuncertain

10 9 8 7 6 5 4 3 2 1
Design and art direction by
Vicky Barker
Additional cover illustrations
by The Boy Fitz Hammond

Manufactured in China,
January 2024
This product conforms to
CPSIA 2008

ISBN
978-1-63158-728-3

WHAT IS AI?

AI stands for **Artificial Intelligence** and it describes a computer
that can solve problems. Computers rely on programmers to write
programs telling them what to do. AI is when a program gives the
computer problem-solving skills that help it make decisions.
Some people think humans will always be better problem-solvers
than computers—and others think that the computers could take over!
What do you think?

WHAT IS STEM?

STEM stands for "science, technology, engineering, and mathematics."
These four areas are closely linked, and can be used to study and make
sense of our world. We need to use the creative thinking skills of an
engineer and the attention to detail of a mathematician to help come
up with new ideas in artificial intelligence.

 Science   Technology Engineering   Math

KEEP IT MOVING

All of us have bodies that move in different ways. Blinking your eyelids is something most people do without thinking about it. But you can also decide to blink when you want to—or even wink, if you can! If a robot had eyes and eyelids, it wouldn't know when to blink unless a programmer told it when—teaching it to do this would be giving it artificial intelligence. This is a type of intelligence that humans have naturally.

This is a robot face that looks very human! Write in each box the things that it will need to know how to do so that people will think it is human.

SENSE YOUR SURROUNDINGS

Making a decision, such as doing some extra blinking, happens after you have sensed the situation you are in. Depending on what senses you can use, you might look at or listen to, touch, taste, or even smell something to learn more about it.

Maybe you can hear or see or feel that it's very windy and there is dust in the air. If a computer needs to interact with the world around it but is not built with **sensors,** then it doesn't know what's happening and can't make a decision. Senses are essential when it comes to this sort of intelligence.

Help this robot learn how to cross the road like a human.
Circle the hazards that it will need to be able to sense.

Answers on page 30.

REMEMBER, REMEMBER

Just as we all have bodies that move in wonderfully different ways, we all have brains that are wired in amazingly different ways too. You might be able to control the way a certain part of your body works and you might be able to sense the situation around you really clearly—but you also need to be able to pay attention long enough to remember what you've sensed and to make a decision (then remember to do it!). This is a really advanced type of intelligence that humans have.

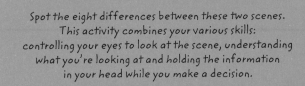

Spot the eight differences between these two scenes.
This activity combines your various skills:
controlling your eyes to look at the scene, understanding
what you're looking at and holding the information
in your head while you make a decision.

Answers on page 30.

9

KNOW-IT-ALL

You've sent a signal to a part of your body, you've sensed your surroundings and you've got a brain that can process the information in its own way. Now what? You need to understand that information! This is called knowledge and you gain knowledge over time by trying new things.

The idea that red means stop and green means go is not just limited to traffic lights. Warning or "danger!" signs are often red too. Green makes you think of nature and safety. Computers need to learn how to divide things into categories so they can build up knowledge. Do you think that's possible?

Look at all of these items carefully. Now close the book!
How many of them can you remember? You can write
them on a piece of paper if you like.

Next take two different colored pens or pencils.
Circle everything to do with lunch in one color and
everything to do with the bathroom in another color.
You have divided the items into two chunks.
Repeat the memory game. Is it any easier?

LET'S PRETEND

Engineers can build machines with sensors and microchips to help receive information and build knowledge. Coders can write programs that give these machines the skills to learn and make decisions. At what point does the machine become as intelligent as a human?

There is one common test inspired by a gifted mathematician, Alan Turing. The test involves a human asking the same question to a computer and a human. If the questioner cannot guess which answer is from the machine, then that machine is thought to be intelligent.

Come up with some questions that you think would confuse a computer.
Remember, the computer can use a search engine so think carefully about what it can and cannot do.

WHAT GOES IN

Computers have inputs and outputs. This means that something goes into the machine—maybe speech through a microphone—and then something comes back out after the input has been processed. The output might be turning the speech to text and displaying it in a document on the computer's screen.

For a computer to be intelligent, a human needs to think about the inputs and outputs necessary to help make something happen.

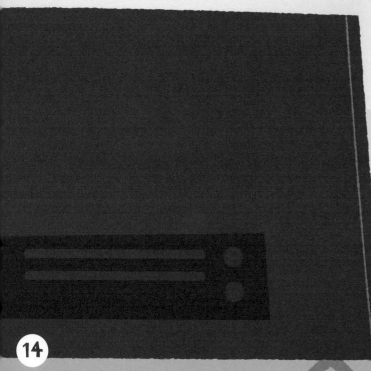

Link these inputs to their outputs so that your AI has the skills to watch your favorite TV show with you. There will be more than one input for each output and answers might be different for different people.

Answers on page 31.

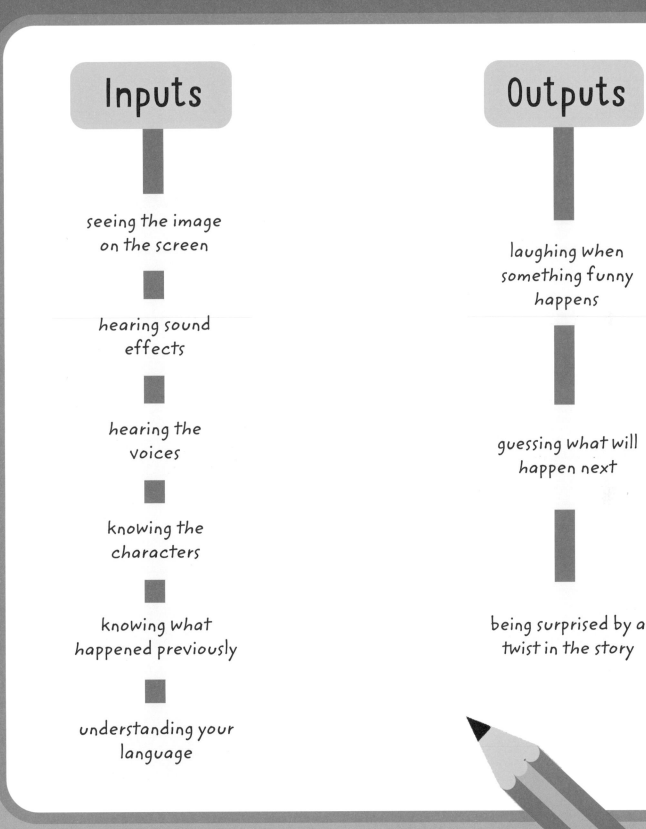

Inputs

seeing the image on the screen

hearing sound effects

hearing the voices

knowing the characters

knowing what happened previously

understanding your language

Outputs

laughing when something funny happens

guessing what will happen next

being surprised by a twist in the story

COMPUTER FAILS

Lots of people are very excited about AI and think it's going to change the way the world works. Other people are less convinced! Some might even be scared about what it can do. Most examples of successful AI show off things that computers are very good at, such as complicated mathematical equations or processing lots and lots of data. But there are many types of intelligence that computers are very bad at, such as emotions or feelings.

AI would find the words hidden in this word search much more quickly than you could. But would they understand what they really mean?

```
d t h f d e r o n g y d e o h v p
y o n u p n t c r i l q j i s v e
k j a t t a n k y o u d o n s n a
c h d i c r u b l e o h g x e n n
a a e g c m i t r d r a e i n t u
b p a h g x e o u a e h s i d l t
d p s t j l q t e s v g h l a e h
e i w g o e u n c t d e l m s u a
e n r x y g s e r y s a d n e h n
f e o r i o p e s i o v u c l n k
h s t u r c v i o g g r u b c e y
i s p a r a e f m n i h g a u t o
c t j u r b c k o t i w t n n t u
d p l e s a f r s z h a a i o u t
a y i v o l w u j a m g o c e y c
s b o r e d o m n i c s c s i k j
g e t c u z y s e o p l e a s e a
```

brave

right

joy

fear

sadness

boredom

happiness

thank you

please

wrong

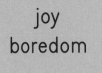

Answers on page 31.

17

FLASH THE PLASTIC

The human brain is very plastic. This means that it can bend and shape itself (not literally!) around ideas and information as it learns. Computers are very static, which means they stay the same unless told otherwise. Machine learning (ML) is one way that engineers and coders are helping computers become more plastic.

ML can have a deep neural network (the term "neural" means related to the nervous system). The engineers give the machine parameters (different options) to help it identify something specific, such as a picture of a puppy. The machine tests itself with lots of different pictures and the deep neural network remembers the results. Over time, it learns how to tell the difference between things that match the right result and things that don't.

The image on the top left here is the one your machine is learning to recognize. Circle the correct parts of the other three images.

Answers on page 31.

ROOTED IN FACT

Another example of artificial intelligence is the decision tree. Human brains work in this way without us even realizing. Instead of asking the computer to look for a right or wrong answer, in this case you want the computer to help you make the best decision for you.

The computer will need to know a little bit about you to be able to help you make a decision. But with the right information, it's possible the computer can tell you what you want before you figure it out for yourself!

Your friend wants to share their lunch with you. This AI can decide whether you should! It knows that you are vegetarian and you don't like tomatoes. Fill in the blank ovals with either

"no, thank you" or "yes, please."

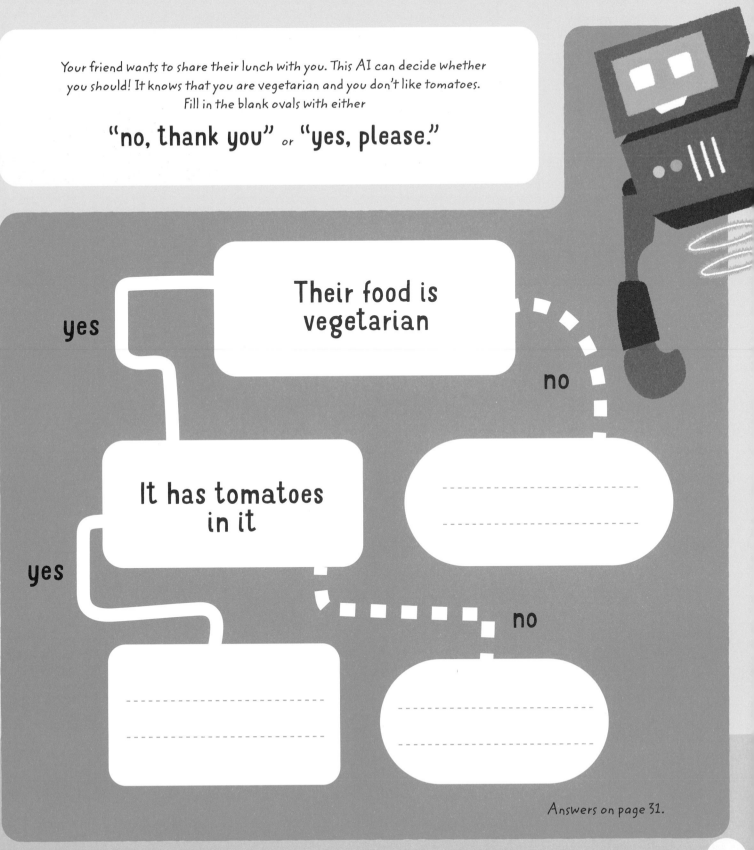

yes

Their food is vegetarian

no

It has tomatoes in it

yes

no

Answers on page 31.

NARROW AI

There are different types of AI and they are sorted into groups based on what they can do. Narrow AI is also known as "weak AI" and it is where the AI can do one very specific task very well. Digital voice assistants are examples of narrow AI. You ask it a question and that's the input. The output is the response, which is created by the machine following lots of rules given to it by coders.

These are very powerful machines that can make us feel like we are talking to a human. But we say they are narrow or weak because they do not really understand what they are doing.

Match the questions with the correct response.

1. What's the weather like today?

2. Will I need a coat today?

3. How long will it take to walk to school?

4. What time do I need to leave?

a. No, you won't!

b. At 8:30am!

c. It's warm and sunny!

d. It will take 15 minutes.

Answers on page 32.

GENERAL AI

If there's a weak AI then is there a "strong AI?" The answer is: not yet! This type of AI is called general AI and for some people it's the ultimate goal. Think about digital voice assistants. They can tell you that it's going to rain later, and they might have learned that rain means you will get wet. They could even know that you love the rain because you told them that at some point and they stored the information.

But if the AI doesn't know this information, it won't think to ask. The idea behind general AI is that it can learn how to do absolutely anything.

Name:

Meet your new AI friend. They have general artificial intelligence! Draw what they look like in the box.
Then fill in all the details about them.

Age:

Height:

Where they are from:

Favorite hobbies:

Favorite food:

Special skills:

NEARLY THERE!

AI based on a large language model (LLM) appears to be very clever. Most computers need their inputs to be exactly right for them to know what to do next. But with an LLM, the input is whatever question you ask it. Since it doesn't know beforehand how you are going to ask the question, it needs to be ready for anything!

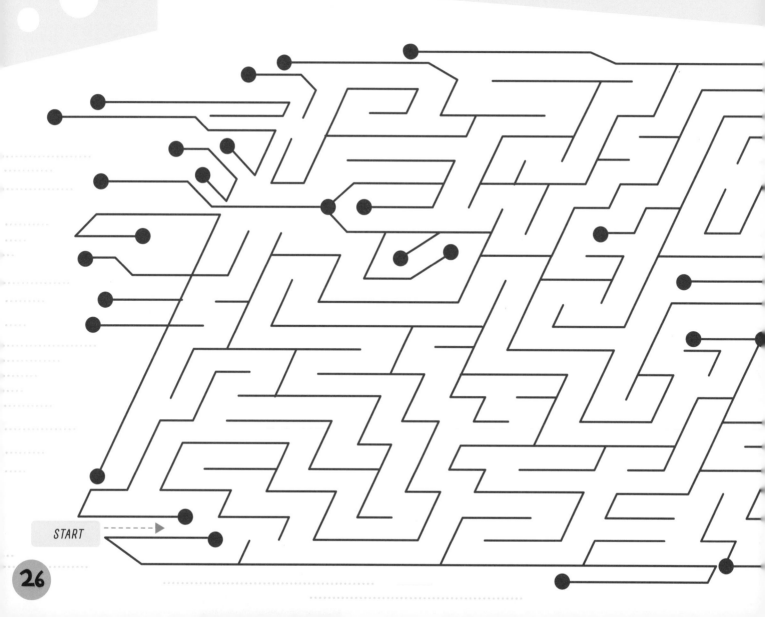

START

The AI uses its language skills to give you an answer in words that you will understand too. Engineers building these models need to train their machine learning with millions, if not billions, of parameters to help the AI understand you and reply.

Send the data through the maze to get to the AI brain.

END

YES! I CAN HELP YOU WITH THAT.

Answer on page 32.

AI IN HISTORY

There is no such thing as an overnight success!
Engineers rely on decades of research by experts
to build new AI models. Here are some famous
examples from history.

Talk to ELIZA

In the 1960s, professor Joseph Weizenbaum created a chatbot called
ELIZA at the Massachusetts Institute of Technology (MIT) in the US.
Users could "chat" to ELIZA by typing their message into the computer.
Weizenbaum had trained ELIZA to recognize key words and reply in an
encouraging or sympathetic way.

He noticed that ELIZA's responses made users feel very
comfortable. They would share personal information
about their worries and fears.

```
EEEEE LL     IIII ZZZZZ  AAAA
EE    LL      II     ZZ  AA  AA
EEEE  LL      II    ZZ   AAAAAA
EE    LL      II   ZZ    AA  AA
EEEEE LLLLL IIII ZZZZZ   AA  AA
```

What a MENACE!

In 1961, British researcher Donald Michie invented the Matchbox
Educable Noughts And Crosses Engine, or MENACE for short, and used
matchboxes to explain. (The game noughts and crosses is commonly known as
"tic tac toe" in the US.) Every possible move in the game was drawn on to a
matchbox. Inside each matchbox were colored beads that told the machine
where to place their circle. Michie played 220 games with MENACE adding
beads to the matchboxes that worked and taking them out of the ones that
didn't. This helped MENACE "learn" the different ways that tic-tac-toe can go.
Eventually, MENACE built a system that could win!

There were 304
matchboxes in total.

Play tic-tac-toe! The first player draws an X in one of the boxes. The second player draws an O in another box. Take it in turns to add Xs and Os. The goal is to get three in a row!

You could make your own tic-tac-toe boards so you can play again and again.

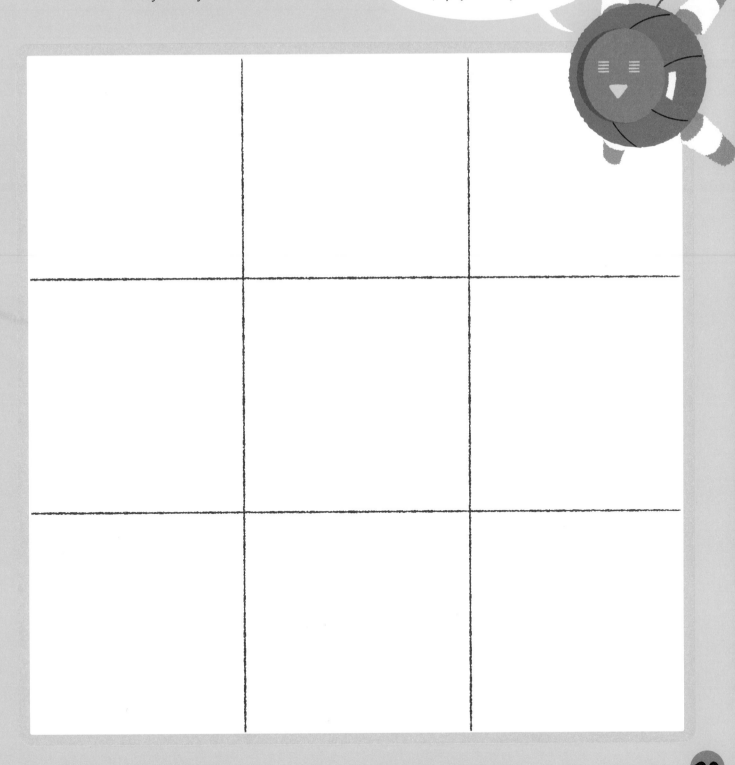

ANSWERS

pages 6-7

pages 8-9

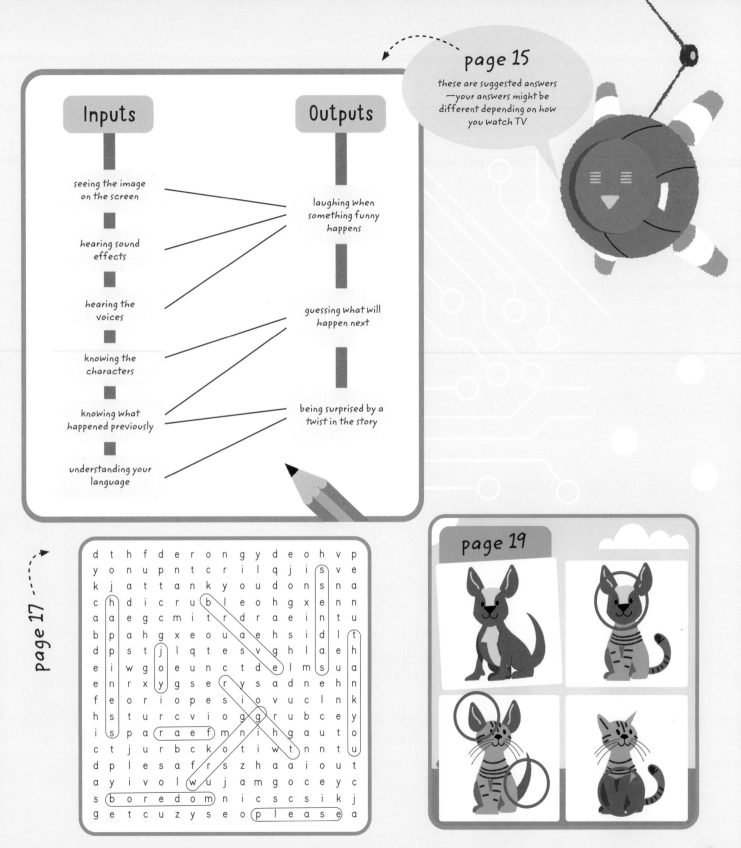

page 15

these are suggested answers —your answers might be different depending on how you watch TV

Page 17

page 19

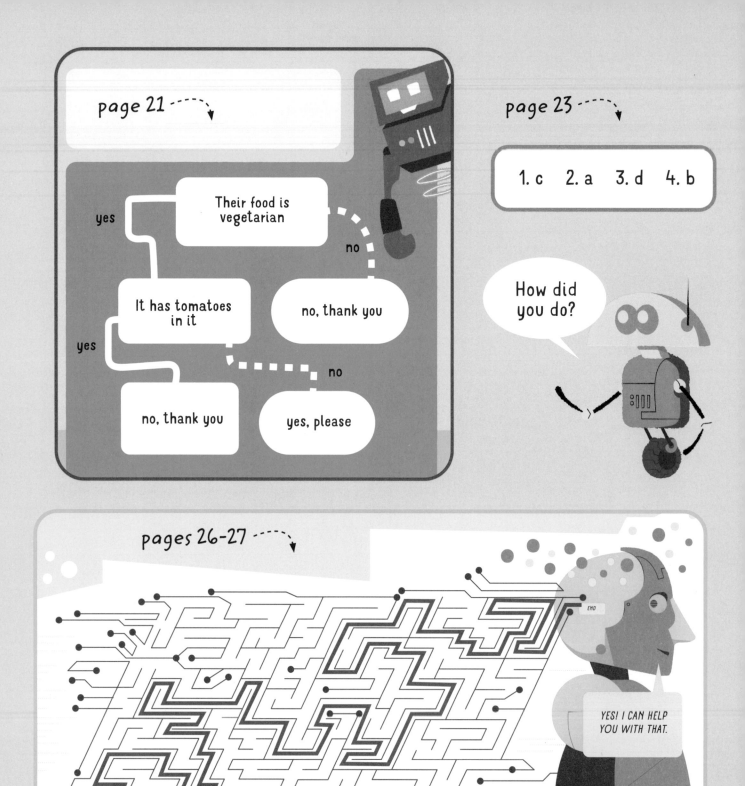

page 21

yes — Their food is vegetarian

no

yes — It has tomatoes in it

no, thank you

no

no, thank you

yes, please

page 23

1. c   2. a   3. d   4. b

How did you do?

pages 26-27

START

END

YES! I CAN HELP YOU WITH THAT.